Behind Gold Doors

Why Did I Say Yes?

Three Steps to Respond Without Guilt

Lonnie Pacelli

Published by Pacelli Publishing
Bellevue, Washington

BEHIND GOLD DOORS
WHY DID I SAY YES?

Published by Pacelli Publishing
9905 Lake Washington Blvd. NE, #D-103
Bellevue, Washington 98004
PacelliPublishing.com

ISBN-13: 978-1-933750-99-6

Check Tire Light

Dang, the Check Tire light is on.

Ken had to get to the airport for his 7 a.m. flight to Orlando, so despite the dashboard warning, he started his drive. It was 4:30 a.m. on a typical February rainy morning in Seattle. The I-405 had light traffic but the few cars on the road were buzzing by, kicking up spray from the wet pavement.

Just go slow, Ken thought as his wipers, even on high speed, couldn't keep up with the downpour. Driving in the rain never used to bother him, but this morning the warning light made him feel uneasy.

Hope the tire's not flat when I get home, Ken thought as he parked the car and walked through the downpour to catch the shuttle to SeaTac airport. The shuttle was filled with people escaping the northwest for warmer climates in Palm Springs, Mexico, and Florida. Ken had decided only two days earlier to make the trip to Orlando to see his brother, Mark, whom he hadn't seen for years. Going to Orlando for a couple of days would kill three birds with one stone: see Mark, get some sunshine, and do some serious thinking about Jan's ask.

Ken boarded the plane. As he approached his aisle seat, he saw a burly man sitting in the middle seat hogging the arm rests.

Oh well, glad I'm not the one in the middle, Ken said to himself.

Big Ask

The flight was pleasant, except for Mr. Armrest Hogger. Ken napped off and on, watched a movie, and played some video blackjack. His meeting with Jan the day before kept running through his mind in the background. What she had asked was big, and Ken was conflicted on what to do.

I love Jan's passion, and she can really use the help, Ken thought. *I'd like to help, but I don't know if I can do it. I don't want to say no because it will probably hurt Jan's feelings. She's such a nice person.*

After an uneventful landing and rental car pickup, Ken enjoyed the sunny drive to his resort near Universal Studios. He and his wife Laura had stayed there a couple of years earlier and loved the summery vibe.

"I'm happy you're going, but am a little jealous about where you're staying," Laura had said when he made the reservation.

"Well, I know you'll have fun this weekend too, Ken said." Laura was attending a women's retreat that weekend, which gave Ken a good opportunity to make the Orlando trip.

Ninth Floor

"Reservation for Avery," Ken said to the young woman at the resort check-in desk.

"Welcome back, Mr. Avery," she said. "Will you be going to the parks during your visit with us?"

"Not this time." Ken had already plotted out the visit. Get some dinner nearby, then an early bedtime. He decided to split his time between Mark's house and lounging at the resort until checkout.

"We've got you on the ninth floor overlooking the pool, Mr. Avery."

"Glad I remembered my swimsuit."

"It's going to be beautiful weather." She gave him his room key and smiled. "Enjoy your stay, Mr. Avery. The elevators are across the lobby to the right."

"Thanks." Ken took the key and began his walk across the lobby. He turned the corner to see six elevators.

Hmm, odd, Ken thought as he looked at the elevator doors. Five of them were traditional brushed steel, but it was the sixth that caught his attention. Its doors were bright gold with a shiny gold knocker at the center of each door. He stood in front of the gold doors, wondering why that elevator was different than the five. The gold doors opened.

"Going to the ninth floor?"

Porter

Ken stood outside the elevator.

"Going to the ninth floor?" the gravelly, low-pitched voice said again. Ken stepped into the elevator where he saw him.

"Ninth floor, right, Ken?"

Ken looked him up and down. Matching burgundy pants and jacket with gold trim and a matching burgundy bellhop hat. His black shoes were so shiny, they reflected the light above. His wrinkled complexion was framed by perfectly combed silver hair. He smiled at Ken, patiently waiting for him to answer as the elevator doors closed.

"Um, yeah, ninth floor," Ken said. "Do I know you?"

"The name's Porter. I've been operating this elevator for years. I was expecting you."

Ken looked him up and down again and looked around at the elevator. Dark wood paneling with a plush green carpet and a chandelier above.

"This looks like something out of the 1940s," Ken said.

"Well, I've been doing the job a long time. Helped a lot of people over the years. I became a porter after the depression, started in the Empire State building. Been all over the world as a porter in some of the most famous buildings. With a name like Porter, guess I was destined to be a porter. I'm Porter the porter, but you can call me Porter."

Porter grinned at Ken; he'd seen this perplexed look on thousands of faces over the years.

"So, we're going to the ninth floor?" Ken asked.

"We'll be there in a jiffy," Porter said. "Making a few quick stops before we get to your floor." The elevator rocked as it began its journey upward.

"Gosh, I don't know," Ken said. "I'd like to go to my room."

"You'll be there in a flash, scout's honor. Just a few quick stops."

"What stops?" Ken asked.

Porter looked Ken in the eye and put his hand on Ken's shoulder. "Ken, I'm here to help you. I know you've been struggling with Jan's ask of you, and I also know that you've struggled with asks like Jan's a lot in the past."

"You know Jan?"

Porter smiled. "Natch. Great person. Very passionate. I also know you don't want to disappoint her."

Ken squinted and gave Porter a skeptical glare. "Really, who ARE you?"

"Relax, Ken, I'm here to help, like I've helped many before you. I'm going to teach you how to respond without guilt, which sometimes means saying no."

"You're going to teach me how to say no?" Ken laughed. "Isn't that like the first word every toddler learns?"

"Well, that may be true, but a toddler doesn't think about the consequences of saying no, nor does he think about how others might feel when he says no. As adults when we say no, we tend to think about how others may react. For some, it's easy to say no to things and not give it a second thought, but for others who don't like to disappoint people, saying no becomes very difficult. You fit into that category, Ken. I want to help you respond without guilt, even if it means saying no."

Ken thought back to other situations where he really didn't want to do something and didn't know how to say no, and the regret he felt after saying yes.

"So, what are we going to do?" Ken asked.

Porter gave Ken a clipboard. "We'll stop at three floors before we get to the ninth floor. Each floor will describe a step in how you decide on your response to an ask, then confidently respond without guilt. I call it the no-guilt plan."

Porter gave him a clipboard that had the following already written on it:

"After we visit each floor, I will ask you to write down what you have learned from each step."

"Gosh, I don't know. I really want to get to my room and collapse."

"Ken, I promise you it will be worth it, and we'll be done in no time. Ready to fly, ace?"

"You're not giving up, are you? Fine let's make it quick."

"Now we're cookin' with gas! You won't be disappointed." Porter pointed to the elevator buttons. "Look here. There are five buttons; the first one is the main level and the last is the ninth floor. The remaining three are where you will learn about each step in the no-guilt plan."

Porter pressed a button and the elevator bucked as it began its ascent.

"Don't worry, he'll come around," Porter said under his breath as he looked upward.

The Ask

"Stop one," Porter said as the elevator came to a stop and the doors opened to a man and woman sitting at a table.

"That's me and Jan at the coffee shop we met at last week!"

Porter smiled, recognizing the bewildered look he'd seen countless times before.

Jan was in her mid-fifties. An intellectual property attorney by trade, she rose quickly through the ranks at her law firm after getting her JD to become one of the firm's youngest partners. After a long, fulfilling career, she decided to embark upon a next journey as CEO of a non-profit focused on helping adults with disabilities gain employment. The mother of an adult son on the autism spectrum, Jan had developed a passion for helping those with physical, intellectual, and developmental disabilities thrive through meaningful work that delivered value to employers and customers.

"Whoa, was someone recording us?" Ken asked.

"It's not like that. No one was recording you. Just listen," Porter said as he pointed to Jan and Ken sitting at the table.

"Two cappuccinos," the server said as she placed two black cups on the table. Each cup was on a black saucer flanked by a small silver spoon and small biscotti.

"Thank you," Jan said as the server smiled and left them.

Jan took a sip of the cappuccino. "Mmm, these are the best in town. Not too much milk, good head of foam, and chocolate sprinkled across the top. My go-to in the afternoon."

"Yup, mine as well, and the biscotti are killer," Ken said.

Jan put her cup down. "Thanks for meeting up with me, Ken."

"Sure. You missing the IP attorney world?"

Jan smiled. "I do miss working with great clients like you. We've done a lot of great stuff together."

"Indeed. You helped us a ton over the years. Saved us a lot of time and money."

"Was happy to do it," Jan said.

"So, how's the new gig?"

"Well, it's already been five years since I left the practice and took the CEO job. I get such a wonderful feeling of gratitude working with those with disabilities and helping them find and retain fulfilling employment. Did you know that 26 percent of Americans have disabilities?"

"One in four, wow," Ken said.

"Here's another for you. Turnover of employees with a disability is 48 percent less than those without."

"Dang, that's good. Turnover at our company is out of control. I'd love to have that kind of stability."

"You're not alone," Jan said. "The numbers are compelling, and the opportunities are out there, but I need help."

"What do you need?"

"I need some people established in their industry to help mentor our clients."

"Your clients?" Ken asked.

"Oh sorry, we call those with disabilities in the program our clients."

Ken took a bite of biscotti as Jan continued.

"You see, we need mentors to help our clients with how to prepare a resume, how to interview, how to onboard into a new position, how to accept rejection, all the things a candidate must do when finding a job. You'd be a great mentor, Ken."

"Me?" Ken asked.

"Absolutely. You have such great compassion for others, you tell it like it is, and you know what it's like to hire great people."

"Hire yes, retain not so much," Ken said as he smiled.

***

Ken and Porter watched from the elevator.

"This is so weird," Ken said as he watched himself from a week ago talking with Jan.

"Yessir," Porter said. "So, what stressed you out about Jan's ask?"

"The time requirement. She wanted eight hours a month. I'm so bleary-eyed busy right now that I don't think I could handle it."

"Maybe not, but why didn't you say no right then?"

"Well," Ken continued. "I guess I wanted to give it more thought and I…"

"You what?" Porter asked.

"I didn't want to disappoint Jan."

"Right, the people pleaser you are," Porter said.

Ken noticed that Jan was getting up to leave. He gave her a quick hug then sat back down.

"Wait, we left at the same time! I didn't sit back down after," Ken said.

Porter smiled. "This is where things can get a bit confusing, Ken. See, this isn't only about what *did* happen, but also what *should* have happened."

"Huh?" Ken asked, a puzzled look on his face.

"Everything you're going to see from this point forward is about how you can intentionally evaluate Jan's ask using the no-guilt plan steps and then decide what to do about it. I know it looks wacky, but trust me, okay?"

"Exactly who are you again, and how is this happening?" Ken became agitated at his situation.

Porter calmly reassured Ken.

"Ken, I promise everything's okay. I've seen this reaction many times and every time things have worked out for the better. Trust me, ace."

Porter put his hand on Ken's shoulder and gave him a warm smile. He felt this strange feeling of warmth come over him with Porter's gentle touch and friendly gaze.

This is so funky, Ken thought to himself.

"Funky, I love that word!" Porter said.

"Wait, you heard what I was thinking? You some kind of mind reader?"

"Trust me," Porter said as he patted his arm.

Ken slowly looked down and took a deep breath. "We're good," he said calmly.

"Now, back to you at the table."

Ken and Porter watched as Ken pulled out a sheet of paper and started writing. "What am I doing?" Ken asked.

"You're on step one in the no-guilt plan, which is understanding the ask."

"But I understood the ask, it was about being a mentor."

"That's right, but in truly understanding the ask there is more to know that can influence your decision. In fact, there are seven distinct components that constitute understanding the ask."

"Seven?"

"That's right. Let's go through each of them. First is a clear and concise statement of what the asker is asking you to do. In this case it appears clear that Jan wants you to be a mentor."

"Right, that's one," Ken said.

Porter continued. "Second, it's about documenting clearly why the ask is important. Jan was very good at articulating the need and some statistics supporting the need."

"She sure was."

"Third is the length of time the asker is wanting you to support the ask. Do you know how long Jan was asking you to be a mentor? One year? Two years? Forever?"

"Um, not sure," Ken said.

"Right. Fourth is the time or money commitment. Jan said eight hours a month, so you got that one."

Ken smiled.

"Fifth is about the consequence," Porter said as he held up five fingers.

"Consequence?"

"Yessir, for you to make a good decision, it's important to understand any realistic consequences to your saying yes or no. There are two factors at play here. The first is in the word *realistic.* I don't believe Jan would do this, but some people exaggerate the positive or negative consequences of saying yes or no to the ask. They might appeal to you with a 'If you don't respond today then something bad will happen' statement. It's meant to make someone feel guilty if they don't act. The second factor is about the consequence if you, Ken, don't act. With Jan's ask, you are qualified to be a mentor, but you are not the only person who can do it. It's not like the program's success or failure in this case hinges on your answer, but Jan may have to find another qualified person if you say no."

Ken paused for a moment then spoke, "Gosh, this is pretty illuminating. I get, 'The sun won't rise unless you act' unrealistic consequence. I just never thought about being qualified versus best qualified. Me being the fixer I am, I jump to the conclusion that if someone asks me to do something, I'm the one best qualified to get it done. Being qualified among others versus being the one best qualified is a huge distinction for me."

Porter grinned. "You're not alone. Fixers like you tend to feel they can do things better than others so they make the leap to being best qualified. Ready to scoot on?"

"Yeah."

"Good. Sixth is about any other factors that would influence your decision. It could be about anything, like the time of day you need to be available or being in-person versus, what's the term you use these days?" Porter said as he snapped his fingers.

"Virtual?"

"Right! Virtual. It's good to get stuff like that down to help you with your decision."

Porter continued. "The seventh and final component is when an answer is needed by. I don't recall you asking or Jan volunteering that information, right?"

Ken looked up as if searching for the answer. "Uh, that's true."

"Now it could be there isn't a specific date she needs an answer, but it's good to clarify any expectation on either yours or the asker's part." Porter paused, then continued. "So, understanding the ask includes seven components, got it?"

Ken thought for a minute. "I think so."

"Good. How about you write them down?"

"Sorry, do you have a pen?"

Porter reached into his coat pocket and pulled out a shiny gold fountain pen.

Gosh, I haven't seen one of these in years, Ken thought as he took the pen.

"The finest back in my day," Porter said.

Ken looked down and smirked. "Right, forgot that you hear my thoughts. Need to be more careful about that."

Ken wrote on the clipboard-backed paper:

THE NO-GUILT PLAN

THE STEPS:

1. UNDERSTAND THE ASK
   - A. WHAT'S THE ASK
   - B. WHY IT'S IMPORTANT
   - C. DURATION
   - D. TIME/MONEY COMMITMENT
   - E. CONSEQUENCES
   - F. OTHER FACTORS
   - G. ANSWER NEEDED BY

"Good work, Ken. Now, ready for the next floor?"

"Why not," Ken said sarcastically.

"Righty oh, here we go!" The doors closed and Porter pushed the button for the next floor. The elevator lurched as it started upward, then quickly came to a squealing halt.

"Here we are," Porter said as the gold doors opened.

"Where am I?" Ken asked.

Boundaries

The doors opened to Ken sitting on a houseboat balcony watching a beautiful summer sunset reflecting off Seattle's Lake Union. The lake was filled with boaters, kayakers and paddleboarders. Gasworks Park was directly across the water with its familiar remnants of a coal gasification plant splotched with graffiti. It was a serene scene with the gentle rocking of the houseboat, glass of Cabernet, and gentle wind coming off the lake. Ken had his laptop open, alternating between typing some thoughts, sipping wine, and taking in the beauty.

Ken recognized the setting. "That's my dad's place! He bought it after mom died. He always loved the idea of living in a Seattle floating home, but my mom would get seasick in a bathtub."

Porter grinned. "You and Mark have a lot of fond memories there, right?"

"We do," Ken said as his voice turned somber. "Mom died when we were both in college. We had a lot of fun there with frat buddies." Ken paused, then looked straight into Porter's eyes. "Wait a minute, how did you know about Mark and I enjoying time there? Do you know my parents?"

"Actually, I knew your mother quite well. We both worked in the same building at Boeing Corporate. She was an outstanding engineer."

"What'd you do at Boeing?" Ken asked.

"You're looking at it," Porter said as he opened up his arms as if presenting himself to Ken. "I helped a lot of the higher-ups there learn how to respond without guilt. Your mom was one of them. You and Mark were knee-high to a grasshopper when we met. She really took the no-guilt plan to heart. One of my best students."

"Hold on, you helped my mom?"

"Yessirree."

Ken didn't speak, waiting for Porter to say more.

"Your mom was a real giver. She always wanted to help. Before you guys were born, she had more latitude to say yes to things, but once you and Mark came along, she struggled with saying yes to too many things and keeping balance with you boys. She and I talked about the no-guilt plan. She totally got it and put it to use right away."

Ken's voice softened. "She was always so great at prioritizing what we needed. I was amazed at how she balanced it all so well. The cancer took her so early."

Porter put his hand on Ken's shoulder. "She was a great woman, your mom. I see so much of her in you. I really think I can help you like I helped her. Shall we continue?"

Ken gathered himself. "Okay."

"Great," Porter said. "Once you understand the ask, the next step is to have clarity on how to evaluate the ask. You need an objective foundation to decide if something deserves your attention. That's what the no-guilt boundaries are about."

"No-guilt boundaries?" Ken asked.

"That's right. When I say the word boundaries, Ken, what specifically does that mean to you?"

Ken thought for a minute. "Well, I guess for me it's whether I have the time to spend on something."

"Well, that's certainly one definition. Time is an important commodity. The difficulty is that boundaries are typically defined by whatever commodity is most precious to a person at a given point in time. If someone is constrained by time, then the amount of time something may take will be the boundary driver. If someone is constrained by money, then money will be how that person defines boundaries. When it comes to responding without guilt, there are seven no-guilt boundaries."

"Seven?" Ken asked.

"Seven. Let's go through them one by one."

Porter continued. "The first boundary is *purpose.* Your purpose is about how you want to be known. Do you have a purpose statement, Ken?"

"Well, I've been trying, but haven't really locked on something I'm excited about."

"You're not alone," Porter said. "So many people don't have a purpose statement. Your mom didn't have one when we first talked. It wasn't until I talked with her about the no-guilt plan that she put some serious thinking into it. You know what her purpose statement was, right?"

Ken thought for a moment, then recalled the framed saying that his mom had above her desk at home.

I will help others to help themselves
and not simply enable them.

"I remember!" Ken said. "I was always amazed at how Mom walked her talk with helping others to help themselves. She came up with that because of you?"

Porter smiled. "Well, you can say I was the one who got her to think about her purpose statement. It took her some time to come up with it, but when she did, it was like the clouds parted, revealing beautiful rays of sunshine."

Ken shook his head. "This is so surreal."

"Surreal but true," Porter continued. "Living by a purpose statement is great, but if you don't have one yet, the no-guilt boundaries can still work. Having a purpose makes it clearer, like it did with your mom. By the way, do you like jazz?"

"Sorry?" Ken asked.

"Jazz music, do you like jazz?"

"I guess."

Porter closed his eyes. "Ah, I had a flashback to when I was working in Vegas back in the seventies. Buddy Rich and his band were playing at the Flamingo. Man, they were tight!" Porter stood there with his eyes closed, rocking side to side as the music played in his head. After a minute he opened his eyes. "Buddy Rich, the best ever," he said as he smiled.

Ken stood there, not sure what to do with the awkward moment.

"Now where was I? Yes, we were talking about purpose. Purpose is about how you want to be known, your personal statement of being." Porter paused for a moment to give Ken time to absorb.

"Ready for the second boundary?" Porter asked.

Ken's intrigue heightened. "Ready."

"Good. The second boundary is *passion.*"

"What's the difference between purpose and passion?" Ken asked.

"Great question. As I said, purpose is about how you want to be known, or your personal statement of being. Passion is about what you can do that aligns to your purpose and addresses something you really care about. Your mom was passionate about helping younger leaders scale up and be leaders of leaders without burning themselves out. She found great joy in helping to grow engineering leaders. She did it within the guardrails of her purpose and gave them tools so they could help themselves. She was also passionate about other areas, such as helping those with disabilities thrive. She did that by helping them to help themselves to the extent they could do so on their own. She had many passion areas, and she used her one purpose statement to help fulfill her passions. Get it?"

Ken looked up and to the right, as if searching for words in his brain. "In thinking about it, I can see the difference between purpose and passion. I would have thought they were one in the same, but your explanation makes sense."

"Dandy. Now on to the third boundary. It's the one many use when deciding how to respond, but don't use completely. It's *time.*"

"Yes, time," Ken said affirmingly. "But what do you mean about not using it completely?"

"Glad you asked. Ken, do you keep a calendar?"

"Yup."

"What kind of things are in your calendar?" Porter asked.

"Business meetings and sometimes personal meetings."

Porter raised a bony finger. "Right, your calendar contains meetings."

"Yes," Ken said confidently.

"Let me ask you, Ken, is your life one hundred percent about meetings, or do you do other things?"

"Of course I do other things."

"Are those things in your calendar?"

Ken paused. "No, not really."

"Why not?"

"Well, I use my calendar for meetings."

"Do non-meeting things take up time?"

"Well, yeah," Ken said.

"If non-meeting things take up time, and you don't put them in your calendar, then how do you know if you have enough time to take on something new?"

The question caught Ken off guard. "I kind of guesstimate in my mind."

"Typical," Porter said. "Time is one of the most frequently cited boundaries, yet so many of my clients don't understand how much margin they have in their schedule. I am a firm believer in the following principle:

If it takes time to do,
then put it in your calendar."

"Sounds like too much work," Ken said.

"Your mom was a master at this, and it wasn't any more work for her at all. She had the discipline to put everything in her calendar so she had a clear understanding of what was taking up time in her life. She called it her life calendar. Her calendar consisted of work and personal meetings, work time to get her job done, activities that she did with you boys and your dad, and anything else that took up time in her day. It was easy for her to see where she truly had time margin to decide whether to say yes to something new. Without a life calendar, it's easy to wrongly estimate how much time you can devote to a new ask."

A life calendar, Ken thought to himself.

"Yes, a life calendar," Porter said.

Ken grinned. "Right--that mind-reading thing."

Porter let out a chuckle. "So, you've got the third boundary; the fourth is pretty straightforward. It's *money*."

"Yup, understand it well," Ken said.

"Maybe," Porter said. "But I want to put this in context of responding without guilt. Like with a life calendar, it's important to know how much money comes in and goes out to determine how much money margin you have. At the same time, I've seen a lot of clients use money as a pacifier to an asker. They don't want to disappoint them, or they want them to go away, so they throw money at the ask. This is not about your personal judgment of whether it's right to give money to an asker or their cause. I am advocating that you think about money along with your purpose and passion. Your mom did this exceptionally well. She gave money to causes that aligned with her purpose and passion, and said no without guilt to those that didn't align. She also was mindful of her money margin when giving to an asker. If she didn't have the margin, she didn't give."

"But Mom was so generous," Ken said.

"She was. She was also intentional. Your mom said no to many asks for money that didn't align with her purpose and passion. She wanted to give joyfully, and for her that meant giving to things she really cared about. She said no plenty of times and did so without guilt because she had her purpose and passion to justify her giving."

"Hmm," Ken said. "I only saw the times she said yes to money asks. Didn't really see when she said no."

"She did, and with a lot of courage."

Ken smiled as he reflected on Porter's use of the word courage. He always saw his mother as a strong woman. Right up until the very end she was comforting others, telling them to remember all the good times.

"Ken? Ken?"

"Sorry, Porter, just thinking about Mom."

Porter smiled. "I know. Great woman. Now we're getting short on time; are you ready to move on to the fifth boundary?"

"Yes."

"Good. This one may be harder to get your head around. It's somewhat related to time but focuses on the intensity of time spent. It's *mental load.* Heard of it?"

"Nope."

"That's okay, here's an analogy. You enjoy biking, right?"

Ken had become numb to Porter seemingly knowing so much about him. "Yeah," he said with a smile.

"Now let's assume you are doing a two-mile bike ride, and your bike only has one speed. The first mile is on flat, smooth pavement. The second mile is a rougher terrain with an eight percent incline. Which mile is going to be more work?"

"The second, of course," Ken responded.

"Right, the second. Let's liken this to mental load. Say an asker wants you to volunteer at an animal shelter. In one scenario, the asker would like you to clean kennels for four hours a week. In the second, you are asked to help nurse sick dogs back to health. Both are important, but the second, working with sick dogs, can carry much more stress. Now let's add other things that you may be dealing with in your life. If you're already mentally consumed with a challenging job, parenting teenagers, and caring for elderly parents, the idea of taking on the extra mental stress of caring for sick dogs may be more difficult than cleaning kennels. Both have the same time commitment of four hours but can have very different effects on your mental wellbeing. Mental load is your combined personal and professional stress level and the impact of taking on additional stress from an ask."

Ken looked down toward the elevator buttons, reflecting on the concept.

"Do you understand, Ken?"

Ken looked up. "Didn't see this one coming."

"Most don't," Porter said. "It's so easy to overlook. Most people only think about giving in terms of time or money, they don't think in terms of the additional stress the giving might bring on. Let's take money as another example. If giving money to an asker is going to create additional stress when it comes to buying groceries, that in and of itself contributes to mental load. If one can give money without worrying about a food budget, then there is little to no mental load impact."

"So how do I know if I'm at mental load capacity?" Ken asked.

"First, it comes with having a good understanding of your life calendar and your budget. Next is looking at all the stressful events adding to your mental load. Then when an ask comes your way, decide how much stress comes with the ask and how it compares to your current mental load level. Then decide if saying yes allows you to stay below your mental load capacity."

A light bulb went on in Ken's head. "I get it. It's not only a function of time or money, but how much incremental stress I'm willing to take on."

Porter smiled. "Well done." Porter looked out the elevator doors at Ken sitting on the balcony. "He's almost done; shall we catch up to him and talk about the sixth boundary?"

"Don't know what's left but go for it."

"The sixth boundary is pretty straightforward. Sometimes when you are asked to do something, there is a duty or mandate that accompanies the ask. The sixth boundary is *responsibilities.*"

Porter reached into his coat pocket, pulled out a cup and saucer, the cup filled with hot coffee.

"Want one?" Porter asked as he reached into his pocket again.

"Er, I'm good," Ken said, smiling as Porter took a sip.

Porter smacked his lips and continued. "With responsibilities, you do something because you've agreed to it, or it's expected of you in your occupation or vocation. For example, if your job description says you are required to participate in fundraising events, you can't say no without violating your employment agreement. You have a responsibility that needs to be fulfilled with the ask."

"Responsibilities, check," Ken said.

"Dandy. Now here's the seventh, and for most people, one of the hardest boundaries. This boundary is one that people pleasers have great difficulty with. It's one where the fear of hurting someone's feelings weighs on them like a ton of bricks. The seventh boundary is *relationships*."

"Ugh, I know where this is heading," Ken said.

"Sure you do. The relationships boundary aligns to your situation with Jan. Sometimes you give time and/or money because of who the asker is as well as what the asker is asking you to do. It could be that you have a strong relationship with the asker and want to help them out. It could also be that the asker has done something for you, and you want to reciprocate. Now, it doesn't mean you automatically do what the asker is wanting. If the asker wants you to do something that is in direct conflict with your purpose, passion, or time/money/mental load constraints, then it's still within bounds to say no. It does mean that relationships must factor into the decision and that who is asking could determine your answer."

Ken thought back to his long-standing relationship with Jan. "Really good point. I can definitely see how the fact that Jan is asking makes a difference in how I respond."

"True," Porter continued. "However, it's important to consider the relationship component, but not to place so much emphasis on it that you resent saying yes to the asker. Relationships need to be balanced with the other boundaries, not considered to the exclusion of the other six."

Ken thought back to other situations where he said yes to a friend only to regret it later. "I was guilted into saying yes, then didn't follow through with my commitment because I didn't believe in the cause and couldn't make the time. Looking back on it, I was under a lot of stress at the time and the ask added to my mental load. Not only did I feel bad, but the asker was upset with me because I didn't follow through."

"Eureka, Ken!" Porter said as he pointed out the elevator doors to see Ken getting up from his balcony chair.

"Where am I going?" Ken asked.

"To our next stop. Before we go, how about you write down the seven boundaries. Do you remember them?"

"Think so," Ken said as he began writing:

THE NO-GUILT PLAN

THE STEPS:

1. UNDERSTAND THE ASK
   A. WHAT'S THE ASK
   B. WHY IT'S IMPORTANT
   C. DURATION
   D. TIME/MONEY COMMITMENT
   E. CONSEQUENCES
   F. OTHER FACTORS
   G. ANSWER NEEDED BY
2. EVALUATE THE BOUNDARIES
   A. PURPOSE
   B. PASSION
   C. TIME
   D. MONEY
   E. MENTAL LOAD
   F. RESPONSIBILITIES
   G. RELATIONSHIPS

"Done well, Ken. Now, how about we see what's next?" Porter pressed a button and the elevator doors whooshed closed. With a jolt, the elevator began its climb.

"How about Louie Bellson."

"Excuse me?"

"Louie Bellson, the drummer," Porter said. "A double bass drum kit pioneer. Played with many of the greats like Duke Ellington, Tommy Dorsey, and Benny Goodman. Was married to jazz singer Pearl Bailey. He'd blow the wig off me!"

"You a drummer?" Ken asked.

"I was pretty good in my day, now I can barely grip the sticks. How I did love playing," Porter closed his eyes, smiled, and gently bobbed his head. The elevator came to a standstill and the doors opened.

"No way!" Ken said.

Decision

"Mom?"

Ken watched in shock from the elevator as his mother walked over to Ken, gave him a gentle kiss on the cheek, and sat down.

"It can't be!" Ken said to Porter.

Porter smiled. "It can and it is."

Ken crouched down against the elevator's back wall, head in hands.

"She died so long ago," he said quietly. "She never even saw me as an adult."

"It was long ago, but she's got something she wants to share with you now." Porter put the cup and saucer back in his coat pocket and crouched down next to Ken. He'd seen this type of reaction countless times before. "How about we let her take things from here and sit back and watch?"

Ken looked up, marveling at himself and his mother as he poured her some wine, the reflection of sunshine dancing in the glass.

***

"How you doing, honey?"

"All good. Been a beautiful summer."

Mom took a sip. "Mmm, so good on a beautiful summer day. What are you working on?"

"You remember Jan, right?"

"I do. Such a smart woman."

"She is. She rose through the ranks at her law firm then decided to do something totally different. She's now CEO of a non-profit that helps people with disabilities."

"How meaningful," his mom said.

"Agree. Well, she asked me to be a mentor to some of her clients. I'd love to do it, but there's so much going on with Laura, the kids, and work that I don't know if I can dedicate the time and do a good job at it. That's what I'm grappling through."

Mom looked down at the sheet of paper and recognized the seven no-guilt boundaries. "I see you already have a good start. How about we talk through the rest of the process? Maybe I can help."

"Could sure use your wisdom."

"Wonderful. I've used this many times to help with difficult asks. It has really saved me a lot of stress and helped me keep my priorities straight. How about I talk you through what I would do, then you decide how or what you might want to do?"

"Great," Ken said.

"Good. The first thing I would do after understanding the ask is look at each boundary area and write out any pros and cons for that boundary area if I said yes. I would write down any positive aspects of how the ask aligned with my purpose. For me, it was easy because I knew my purpose of helping others to help themselves. So, I wrote out the ways the ask aligned with my purpose statement as pros. Then I wrote out how the ask did not align with my purpose statement. Those were the cons. I then did the same for the other boundaries: passion, time, money, mental load, responsibilities and relationships."

"Yup, pretty straightforward," Ken said.

"It is, but this next step was always crucial for me. For each boundary, I made a yes, no, or not applicable decision as if I were evaluating the ask using only that boundary. One time, I received an ask that only involved giving of my time. For the time boundary, I looked at the pros and cons that I had already written down and, in this case, decided that, based on time only, I could not support the ask. So, the time boundary was no. Because the ask only involved time and not money, the money boundary decision was not applicable. When I was done with the boundaries, I had pros and cons for each boundary, and either a yes, no, or not applicable for each."

"I get it, but how about your final decision?" Ken asked.

"This is the third step in the no-guilt plan. There are four components to the decision: your final decision, alternate idea, revisit date, and decision explanation."

Mom took a quick sip, closed her eyes and slightly smiled. "That's such a good wine," she said. "Ok, now where were we? Right, the four components. The first one is the final decision. This is simply one of four choices, yes, no, not now, or alternate idea. Your input into this decision is the pros, cons and decision information that you wrote down for each boundary area. A yes decision means you can support the ask. A no decision means you can't support it, a not now means you'd like to support it but now is not a good time, and an alternate idea decision is that you can't support the ask as presented but you have another idea which may be helpful to the asker."

"You know," Ken said, "as a binary thinker, I typically thought only in terms of yes or no. That's how I would have responded. Not now and alternate idea are new ways to think about the decision."

Mom put her wineglass down. "They are, and honestly, they both make good sense. There's no law that says you can only respond to an ask with a yes or no. Not now allows you to acknowledge your support of an ask, but tells the asker that now is not a good time and that you will revisit your decision in the future. Alternate idea also acknowledges support but proposes another way you can support the asker that better aligns to your boundary analysis."

"Makes sense," Ken said.

Mom continued, "Let's move to the next component. If your decision is alternate idea, this is where you spell out what the alternate idea is. If someone is asking for time and you can't carve it out in your schedule, then you may propose donating money. It's a way of supporting the asker in a way they didn't originally intend. The alternate idea may not be ideal for the asker, but it provides support with less stress. It also doesn't have to be a significant time or money decision. It could be something like posting something in a storefront, providing an endorsement for a website, or donating a product for an auction. It's constrained only by your creativity."

"I really like the alternate idea," Ken said. "I already have some ideas on how I could use this with Jan's ask."

"Glad you're thinking this way, Mr. Binary Thinker," Mom said with a smile.

"Now on to the revisit date. If your decision was yes, not now, or alternate idea, be sure to have a date in mind to revisit your decision. For a not now, this is the date you would decide if the not now could turn into a yes or alternate idea. Now this next part is really important. If your decision was yes or alternate idea, you need to set an expectation of when you will revisit the decision whether to continue. Let's say you agreed to be a mentor in Jan's organization. Saying yes doesn't necessarily mean that you do it forever; there needs to be some review rhythm to re-evaluate your decision based on the seven boundaries and decide whether to continue. You could decide after six months or a year that other more important things are taking up your time and you need to back off on your support. It's crucial that, when you make a decision other than no, you set expectations with yourself and the asker as to how long you will support the ask and when you intend to revisit the decision. The timeframe could be one, three, or six months, or whatever, but make sure you're comfortable with the commitment period and that you give yourself an offramp if your boundaries change."

"Gosh, I can see how the revisit date is such an important but overlooked component," Ken said. "Setting expectations with the asker up front is crucial for minimizing hurt feelings or resentment. I typically say, 'Sure, I'll support you,' without any expectation of when or if I may change course later."

Mom nodded her head in agreement. "Before I understood the guilt-free plan, I was horrible at setting revisit date expectations. There were times when I either continued something longer than I really wanted, or if I did stop supporting an ask, created a situation where the asker was hurt or upset with me."

"I can't imagine anyone getting upset with you, Mom."

She smiled. "Believe me, it has happened more than once. Ready for the fourth component?"

"Yup."

"The fourth is the decision explanation. This is where you decide how to respond to the asker. If the answer is a yes or not now, then you respond as such with a date you will revisit your decision. If the answer is alternate idea, then you respond with the alternate idea and a date in which you will revisit your decision. If the answer is no, then say no with only as much qualification as you want to provide. Suppose someone wants you to contribute money to a social, political, or religious cause that doesn't at all align with your purpose or passion. You can decide how little or how much detail to go into to justify your answer. Here's a guideline I use: ensure your justification is about the ask and not the asker. If the asker supports a cause I don't believe in, then I explain my no based upon the cause, not on the character of the person asking about the cause."

"But what if the reason for saying no IS about the person?" Ken asked.

"Good question. In step one, your job is to understand the ask. If the asker doesn't have the established credibility or integrity to make the ask in the first place, then saying no at that point is totally within bounds. How many telemarketer calls do you get where someone you don't know is asking you for money? It's unreasonable to expect that for every call you get, you'll go through the no-guilt plan steps before providing an answer. It will likely be a no answer right away, either explicitly or by hanging up. Understanding the ask means not only validating the ask but ensuring the asker has the integrity and credibility to make the ask."

"Great point, Mom. Some good stuff to think about."

"How about some crackers and cheese?" She said as she got up and kissed Ken on the forehead. "I love you, honey."

***

Ken stared at the balcony scene, eyes welling, as the elevator doors closed.

"Fine woman, your mom was," Porter said, still crouched down next to Ken.

Ken wiped away a sniffle. "The best."

Ken stood and helped Porter get up from the crouched position.

"Whoa, these legs are creakin'!" Porter said as he regained his balance. "So, what do you think about step three?"

"She explained it so well, like she did everything."

"That she did. You know, when I helped your mom way back when, she said the same about her dad."

"You knew gramps?"

"Sure did, met him in an elevator in Dublin before he came to America. He had the same discussion with your mom sitting on a park bench at St. Stephen's Green. She and I watched from the elevator as he told her about step three. Her reaction was identical to yours."

"Hold on," Ken said. "Gramps died an old man when I was a baby. How old are you?"

Porter smiled. "Can you remember step three enough to write it down?"

"Definitely." Ken wrote on the clipboard:

THE NO-GUILT PLAN

THE STEPS:

1. UNDERSTAND THE ASK
   A. WHAT'S THE ASK
   B. WHY IT'S IMPORTANT
   C. DURATION
   D. TIME/MONEY COMMITMENT
   E. CONSEQUENCES
   F. OTHER FACTORS
   G. ANSWER NEEDED BY
2. EVALUATE THE BOUNDARIES
   A. PURPOSE
   B. PASSION
   C. TIME
   D. MONEY
   E. MENTAL LOAD
   F. RESPONSIBILITIES
   G. RELATIONSHIPS
3. MAKE YOUR DECISION
   A. YOUR FINAL DECISION
   B. ALTERNATE IDEA
   C. REVISIT DATE
   D. DECISION EXPLANATION

"Now, on to the ninth floor!" The doors closed and the elevator continued upward.

"What about Neil Peart?" Porter asked.

"The drummer from Rush? You heard of him?"

"I may be old, but I still appreciate talent. One of the best ever. Nicknamed The Professor. An amazing drum kit. He was a one-man percussion orchestra."

Ken smiled, looking at this quirky man with the perfectly combed silver hair and burgundy coat and slacks. *Why is he here?* he thought to himself.

"To live up to a promise," Porter said.

"A promise?"

"Yessir. Your mom knew how soft-hearted you are, and she knew you'd have problems saying no to things. I promised her that I would do for you like I did first for your grandfather then for her. I didn't think until today you were ready to hear it. In fact, I half-thought you were going to tell me it was a bunch of gobbledygook. I'm thankful you listened; your mom and grandfather will be so proud of you."

"Wait, you're going to see them?" Ken asked.

Porter smiled, then continued. "Oh, I almost forgot, I have something for you." Porter reached into his coat pocket and handed Ken a pin.

"This is a reminder of the no-guilt plan and using it when you're faced with a tough ask."

The elevator stopped and the doors opened to a long hallway of hotel rooms.

"Ninth floor!" Porter said. "Be seein' ya!"

Ken walked out of the elevator and turned as the doors started to close.

"Porter, tell them I love and miss them both."

The elevator's gold doors started closing.

"I will, and don't worry about the Check Tire light."

Porter's wrinkled face smiled as the doors closed. Alone in the elevator, he looked upward and said, "You're welcome."

Ken went into his room, collapsed on the bed, reached for the TV remote, and turned it on, where he saw a Buddy Rich clip from the seventies playing on TV.

"Huh," Ken said. He looked down at the pin, two tiny gold doors like the elevator's. He put the pin on his backpack.

Next Morning

Ken tossed and turned all night, then finally got up at 6 a.m. He couldn't stop thinking about Porter, the gold-door elevator, and the unbelievable journey to the ninth floor. Seeing his mother, not aged a bit, despite her dying decades ago, talking with her as if it were yesterday.

I was cheated out of so much time with her, he said to himself. *How could this have happened? A who-knows-how-old elevator operator in an antique elevator, talking about Mom and Gramps? Saying he taught them about the no-guilt plan? It's too much to take in.* Then he looked at his backpack with the gold doors pin on it and the clipboard resting alongside.

I don't understand it, but the pin and clipboard are proof it happened. Ken got up, showered, dressed, and made a cup of coffee. He went out onto the hotel room balcony with his computer and the clipboard. He then went through each of the three no-guilt plan steps.

Step one, understand the ask. He realized that, despite his conversation with Jan, he didn't truly understand everything about the ask. He shot off an email to Jan with questions about the duration, consequence, whether there was anything else Jan wanted to communicate about the ask, and when the answer was needed by. Jan, being an early riser, responded right away. Feeling like he had a good understanding of the ask, he then moved on to the boundaries. He hadn't yet developed a purpose statement so couldn't assess the pros and cons.

Work on my purpose statement, Ken put on his to-do list.

The ask didn't quite align with Ken's passions, but there was nothing in the ask that was conflicting. To gauge the time commitment, he added non-meeting and personal items into his calendar to make it more of a life calendar, then tried to fit the time commitment in. Eight hours a month simply wasn't going to work out. Jan wasn't asking for money, though Ken did think giving a donation could be an alternate idea. He was already under a lot of work stress, and he felt the incremental stress would exceed his mental load capacity. It wasn't his duty to say yes, so the responsibilities boundary wasn't a factor. He did place a very high value on his relationship with Jan and wanted to try to help her out as best he could.

He looked at his pros, cons and decisions for each boundary area for about fifteen minutes.

I know exactly what to do, he thought, and started furiously typing.

He left his room and headed toward the elevators, all six with brushed steel doors.

Hmm, where's the gold door elevator? he asked himself.

He stopped at the concierge desk in the lobby.

"Excuse me?" Ken asked the concierge.

"How can I help you, sir?"

"Is Porter here today?"

"I'm sorry?"

"Porter, the elevator porter, is he on shift?"

"Sorry sir, we don't have any elevator porters, and we don't have anyone named Porter who works at the hotel."

Ken was silent, with a puzzled look on his face.

"Is there anything else I can help with?" the concierge asked.

"Um, no, thanks," Ken said as the concierge turned his focus to another guest.

Weekend with Mark

Ken drove north on I-4 for the thirty-minute trip to Mark's house.

Do I even tell Mark about Porter and seeing Mom? he thought as he drove past the building they used to call The I-4 Eyesore on his way to Longwood. *Let's see how things go this weekend.*

"Hey, Ken!" Mark said after he opened the door.

"Good to see you, bro!" Ken hugged Mark as he stepped inside.

"How was the flight?"

"Sat next to Mr. Armrest Hogger. Fortunately, I wasn't in a middle seat."

"I've been there," Mark said. "You're staying at a great place. Anything exciting happen at your hotel?"

Ken paused for a moment. "Nope, normal night."

Ken and Mark had a great weekend chit-chatting, catching up on family members, and gossiping about a few. A couple of times Ken wanted to tell Mark about Porter and seeing their mother but decided to keep things light. The story was so implausible that Mark likely wouldn't have believed it anyway.

On his last day in town, Ken stopped to see Mark one more time before driving to the airport to go home. As they said their goodbyes, Mark spotted the gold pin on Ken's backpack.

"Hey, where did you get that pin?" Mark asked.

Ken smiled. "From an old friend."

"I can't place it, but I think I've seen one of those before," Mark said to himself as Ken pulled out of the driveway.

The flight back to Seattle was a pain. Ken missed his connection in Charlotte and arrived in Seattle six hours later than planned. He got to his car and turned the key. The Check Tire light briefly flashed then faded to black.

"Thanks, Porter," Ken said to himself as he left the parking lot.

Alternate Idea

"Thanks for meeting up again, Ken," Jan said as she sat down at the coffee shop they met at two weeks earlier.

"You bet. All still good in CEO-land?"

Jan smiled. "Same grind, but very fulfilling."

"I hear ya," Ken said. "Hey Jan, I wanted to get back to you on the mentoring ask."

"Certainly."

"I actually put a lot of thought into it, along with the help of an old friend. Thank you for helping me better understand the ask. I can see how important it is to get the right mentors in place to help your clients. I went through something called the no-guilt plan. . ."

Jan interrupted, "I understand if you have to say no."

"Actually, I have an alternate idea. When I looked at the impact your ask would have on my time and mental load, I recognized that I couldn't give you the focus you deserve. In addition to my own load, I've got a brother in Orlando I want to make more time for. Because I place a high value on our friendship, I want to propose another idea to you. I talked with two of my directors who are passionate about those with disabilities. They would both like to serve as mentors for you. I told them they could try it for six months then revisit the decision. I know it's not me, but you'll get two people who are every bit as competent and passionate. I'll pay them for their time so they can mentor during work hours. Would that work?"

"So, I get two mentors that you will be funding?" Jan asked.

"That's right."

"And we revisit again in six months?"

"Yup."

Jan paused for a moment. "Well, I'd always love to have your mindshare, but your offer of two of your folks to help me as mentors is terrific. Of course it would work!"

"Great. Their names are Ali and Marya. I'll send an email introducing you to them and you can take it from there. Good?"

"Good."

They chatted a few more minutes, then stood and hugged before leaving the coffee shop. As Ken was walking to his car he saw across the street the back of a silver-haired man wearing burgundy pants and jacket with gold trim and a matching cap.

"Porter?" Ken yelled.

The man turned and winked his wrinkled eye at Ken right before a bus drove between them. When it passed, he was gone.

Two Years Later

"Can I help with that box?" Ken asked.

Mark and Ken were cleaning out their father's floating home, getting it ready for sale. The boats on Lake Union slowly passed by, each leaving a gentle wake to not disturb the paddleboarders.

In the two years since Ken met Porter, he had used the no-guilt plan many times, using the yes, no, not now, and alternate idea decisions about equally. He taught it to his leadership team, including Ali and Marya, who in turn taught it to their teams.

He immediately went to work to define his purpose statement; he decided to adopt his mother's purpose statement since it fit him so well. He felt so much better about those things he said yes to, was more confident in those things he had to say no or not now, and loved being creative with alternate ideas. Using the no-guilt plan was life-changing.

"I found this box; it looks like it's Mom's stuff," Mark said. "How about we grab some iced tea and sit on the balcony?"

"Sounds great," Ken said. "And bring Mom's box."

"Sure thing."

For Ken it was almost a déjà vu moment from his elevator ride with Porter when he was shown the scene of himself and his mother sitting in the same spot. Ken opened the box. In it were some cards and memorabilia the boys had made for her when they were young, then Ken pulled out her organizer. He thumbed through her calendar, looking at how diligent she was at filling it with both work and personal things.

"She really lived by a life calendar," Ken said.

"She did. Hey, I'm getting some pretzels. Want some?" Mark said.

"Love it," Ken said as Mark left the balcony for the kitchen. Ken continued to sort through the box, then saw something in the corner.

Hey, what's that? Ken thought as he reached in with two fingers. He pulled out two gold door pins.

Ken smiled, grabbed his backpack, and pinned the two pins next to his.

Get the no-guilt plan template and other resources at ***BehindGoldDoors.com***.

See a sample chapter from *Behind Gold Doors-Nine Crucial Elements to Achieve Good-Enough Contentment*

At This Time...

Ty got his morning coffee and turned on his computer. The first email was from one of the companies where he had sent his resume. He hovered the cursor over the email, took a deep breath, and double-tapped the track pad, opening the email.

Dear Mr. Taylor:

Thank you so much for your interest in Lake Industries. At this time...

Ty closed the email without reading further. They all started out with something like "*at this time,*" "*unfortunately,*" *or* "*we currently don't.*" They ended with an empty "*we will keep your resume on file should something become available which matches your skillset. Thank you for your interest in blah-di-blah company.*" He had gotten dozens of them, each one like a slug to the gut. Just as he shut his laptop Kate came into the kitchen. She immediately could tell what had happened.

"I'm so sorry, Ty," Kate said as she came around to him and put her hand on his shoulder. "Something will turn up; you just need to be patient."

Ty took a sip of coffee. "It's been six months and not one bite. Severance is gone, and the pittance we get from unemployment runs out next week. How much more patient do I need to be?"

"I wish I knew, honey. We're doing okay on finances and I've got plenty of client work in backlog. We've been through tougher times than this and we got through it. We'll get through this too." Kate poured herself a cup of coffee in a travel mug and took her lunch out of the fridge. "We'll talk more tonight, honey; I believe in you."

"I'm so lucky to have you," Ty said. "Do you want a lift to the train station?"

"I'll walk this morning, but how about you pick me up tonight? I should be on the 5:40, I'll call you if not."

"Got it, I love you."

Kate leaned over to kiss Ty. "Love you too."

Kate headed down the hallway to the front door. Ty heard the door open then gently click shut as she left.

His routine was the same every day. After Kate left for work, he'd finish going through his email inbox, then cruise the news websites, then up for a shower, then onto the job websites. As the weeks went by and the rejections piled up, he cast his job search net wider and wider; even looking at jobs that new college grads could do. He spent hours each day looking at opportunities, trying to network, and responding to job postings. Sometimes after lunch he would break routine and just sit on the couch with a bowl of chips watching afternoon talk shows. The couch sessions increased in frequency as he became more and more depressed. Most times he just wore sweats, since his pants had become too tight, but he knew better than to wear something with an elastic waistband if he and Kate were going out. He'd do the best he could to squeeze into his pants, preferring hooks over snaps to avoid them popping under pressure.

Socializing with friends was the worst. "How's the job search coming?" He'd hear it over and over. "Just great, pursuing a couple of opportunities," he'd lie, then try to change the topic. He particularly hated having to face his daughters and his shame of feeling like such a loser-unemployed dad.

Ty finished up his morning activities then made himself a tuna sandwich with chips and soda. "Wonder what's on TV this afternoon?" he said. "No, I need to work." He looked at his laptop, then the TV remote, then back at the laptop. "Actually, I need to get out." He finished his lunch, got his jacket and left the house for a walk.

"It's a beautiful Fall day," Ty said to himself as he walked down the street towards the train station. It was about a mile walk, one that he used to do every day when he worked at Conset, and the same that Kate did each day to get to her office. The street was lined with reddish-yellow trees that rained leaves onto the ground with each gust of wind. Ty took deep breaths as he walked, feeling the cool Autumn air fill his lungs. He walked by the park next to the train station. Two mothers with strollers sat on a bench talking. A man played fetch with his dog; on each throw the dog would run as fast as he could to the ball, kicking up a trail of leaves with each lunge. As he got closer to the train station, he noticed an old woman sitting in a wheelchair next to a bench. He slowed his walk to look at her. She wore a huge hat adorned with white flowers, a pink polka-dot sweater, and red and orange striped pants. On her lap sat a large paisley-print carpet bag. Her makeup looked as if it were applied with a putty knife. Her sunken eyes stared at Ty as he walked by, expressionless in her gaze, even though Ty smiled at her as he passed. As he continued to the station, he turned to look at the woman, who was still ogling him. Ty quickened his pace to get out of her eyeshot.

"Think I'll go into the city," Ty said to himself as he arrived at the train station. "I can make the 1:05, get into Chicago by 2, then Kate and I can ride the 5:40 back together.". He loved walking along Lakeshore Drive and experiencing the sights, smells and sounds of the expansive Lake Michigan. He bought a ticket and waited on the platform for the train to Union Station. The train's horn broke the silence of the Fall day as it approached the station; followed by the grinding of the metal wheels on the track as the train slowly approached the platform. He stood to board the train as it came to a stop. "How odd," he said to himself. The car was a familiar dingy silver, weathered by the countless trips around Chicagoland. What wasn't so typical were the doors--gleaming gold, looking as if they were just delivered from the foundry and installed that day. The doors slid open, Ty boarded, then with a whoosh the doors closed behind him. He looked up and down the empty car and sat down in the seat next to the doors. Ty pulled out his phone, waiting for the train to depart. Just then the door abruptly opened.

"Help me!" Ty heard as he turned and looked back at the door.

See a sample from *Behind Gold Doors-Five Legends Offer the Keys to Empowering Leadership*

Embossed Card

Sam had been dreading this meeting for days. He stood outside Karen's office waiting for her to finish her phone conversation. He could see her through the window in her door. She held up her index finger. Only one more minute before the dressing-down.

Karen hung up the phone and motioned Sam in.

"How's it going?" Sam said.

"Fine, thanks."

Karen got up from her desk and sat at a small round table with two chairs. Sam sat across from her and put his notebook and water bottle on the table.

"Sam, have you had a chance to review your performance appraisal?"

Sam opened his notebook. In it was a folded copy of the appraisal.

"I have."

"Good. Let's talk through strengths and areas for improvement."

Sam had always been an over-achiever. Graduating from college at age 20, he took great pride in how much he achieved at such a young age. He had been considered a rising star at the company since joining five years earlier. He was recently promoted to a management position, with an organization of ten people reporting to him. This was his first performance appraisal as a manager.

"So, let's first go through strengths," Karen said. Sam barely looked at the strengths, it was that one area for improvement that dominated his thoughts.

Karen continued. "Great delivery results, you come in on budget, customer satisfaction exceeds expectations. Great work." Karen continued with more specifics and comments from customers. Sam sat quietly as she talked, giving an occasional nod and *mm-hmm* to signal understanding.

"Enough with this, get on with the meat," he thought.

"Great, now let's talk about areas for improvement."

Sam leaned back in his chair, his hands gripping the armrests.

"Your organization's employee satisfaction surveys raised something we need to work on together."

Sam looked back at his manager score on the appraisal where his score was compared to other managers in the company. His score was among the lowest, with 95 percent of the managers scoring higher than him. It was the first time in his career he wasn't at the top of the heap, let alone being in the lowest five percent.

"In looking at the questions and comments, people seem concerned about your ability to empower others."

This was a total shock to Sam. He thought he did a great job of delegating and getting things done with his team. It wasn't just one person who said he didn't delegate effectively; it was a consensus among his team.

"I just don't understand this," Sam stammered. "I work so hard to make sure I am delegating work effectively." Karen and Sam continued to talk through the employee survey. To Karen, this was something for Sam to work on in his leadership journey. To Sam, it was like having bamboo stuck under his fingernails. Karen saw how this was impacting Sam; so she decided to make him an offer.

"Sam, you have great potential, and I want to ensure I'm doing my part to help you grow as a leader." Karen got up from the table, went back to her desk, opened the top drawer, took out a gold card, and sat back down at the table.

"There is a very special empowerment class I would like you to attend," Karen said as she handed him the card.

Sam looked at the card, a gold embossed door on the front, an address on the back. He recognized the address.

"This is a bakery; you want me to go to a class at a bakery?"

"Take tomorrow off. Go to the address on the card. They'll be waiting for you."

"Um, okay," Sam said. He had thought for sure he would be fired. Instead he was being sent to a class. Sam got up from the table, grateful he still had his job but perplexed by the gold card and what awaited him the next day.

"Thank you, Karen."

"Hang in there Sam, and let's get together after the class to talk about what you've learned."

"Okay." Sam left her office. As he walked to his office, he ran his thumb over the outline of the door on the embossed card. He flipped it over and looked at the address again.

"A bakery?"

See a sample from *Behind Gold Doors-Seven Steps to Create a Disability Inclusive Organization*

Rain Gear

For the rest of the day Jade couldn't get Kelly's story out of her mind. She had never known anyone close to her with a disability and couldn't imagine the pain Kelly felt watching her father die the way he did.

"*How could I possibly do this justice?*" she thought to herself. "*I'm an engineer, I build stuff. I don't have the experience to do this. What if I fail? I don't want to disappoint Kelly, knowing how important this is to her.*" Jade got up to get some water. On the way she looked outside at the dark clouds forming. "*Gonna need the rain gear tonight,*" she thought.

At 5:30 p.m. she packed up her stuff, slipped on her rain pants and jacket, and headed out. She walked by Kelly's office just as Kelly looked up and gave Jade a quick wave goodbye.

It was unusually dark for this time of year. The rain quickly went from a light mist to a torrential downpour. Jade had ridden in rain before, but nothing quite like this. "*Just go slow,*" she thought as she went through each intersection. She considered stopping and waiting it out, but there was no guarantee that it would let up. "*Halfway home. I can do this.*"

Then it happened.

Acknowledgements

Behind Gold Doors: Why Did I Say Yes? was a fun book to research and write. Heartfelt thanks to Kayla Down, Keith Krell, Sam Lake, Darran Littlefield, Trevor Pacelli, Mike Sanders, and Spencer Stumpf. Special thanks to my editor and wife Patty Pacelli for the hours of reading, reviewing, cleaning up my bad English, and wise counsel. Each contribution made the manuscript more interesting and credible. My deepest thanks to each of you.

More Books by Lonnie Pacelli

Want to be a leader others admire? Get the 12 simple leadership lessons the best leaders crush in *Why Don't They Follow Me?*

Want to be more disability inclusive but don't know where to start? You need the seven steps in *Behind Gold Doors-Seven Steps to Create a Disability Inclusive Organization*

Need to deliver projects on time, budget, and within scope? Get 100 lessons to make you a better project manager in *Six-Word Lessons for Project Managers*

Want to know how to avoid the project guillotine? Get 100 lessons to avert failure in *Six-Word Lessons to Avoid Project Disaster*

Want to know what it really means to be a great project sponsor? See how and more in the *Project Management Screw-Ups Series*

Are you guilty of the seven deadly sins of leadership? See this and more in the *Straight Talk Leadership Seminars*

Want to be the type of leader who people *want* to follow? Get 75 lessons the best leaders use to deliver results in *Lead Already!*

See Lonnie's Amazon Backlist at LonnieOnAmazon.com.

See more about Lonnie at LonniePacelli.com

www.ingramcontent.com/pod-product-compliance
Lightning Source LLC
LaVergne TN
LVHW051017080826
845145LV00009B/2676
9781933750996